CLIMATE CRISIS

Ocean Life

Stephen Aitken

Cavendish Square
New York

Special thanks to Jamison Ervin, a conservation specialist and a project manager with the United Nations Development Programme, for her expert review of this manuscript.

Published in 2014 by Cavendish Square Publishing, LLC
303 Park Avenue South, Suite 1247, New York, NY 10010

First Edition

Library of Congress Cataloging-in-Publication Data
Aitken, Stephen.
Climate crisis : ocean life / Stephen Aitken.
p. cm.— (Climate crisis)
Includes bibliographical references and index.
Summary: "Provides information on how climate change affects ocean life"—Provided by publisher.
ISBN 978-1-60870-460-6 (hardcover)
ISBN 978-1-62712-040-1 (paperback)
ISBN 978-1-60870-631-0 (ebook)
1. Ocean—Juvenile literature. 2. Marine ecology—Juvenile literature. 3. Climatic changes—Juvenile literature.
I. Title.
GC21.5.A35 2012
577.7'22—dc22
2010025510

Editor: Megan Comerford
Art Director: Anahid Hamparian
Series Designer: Nancy Sabato

Photo Research by Laurie Platt Winfrey, Carousel Research, Inc.

Cover: Media Bakery/Colossus Value

The photographs in this book are used by permission and through the courtesy of: *Alamy*: Photoshot Holdings, 1; Mike Grandmaison/First Light, 4; Mark Conlin, 8-9; Daniel Kobb, 17; Ton Keone/Picture Contact, 31; Russell Millner, 32-33; Martin Shields, 50-51. *Center for Microbial Oceanography: Research and Education, adapted from NASA image*: 7. *Getty Images*: Ove Hoegh-Guidbert/AFP, 18. *Glow Images*: Anopdesignstock, water details: 3, 15, 20, 30-31, 38, 40, 55, 57, 60, 62, 64. *©Martin Hartley*: 35. *iStockPhoto*: Earth model: 3, 5, 57, 60, 62, 64. *Illustration © John MacNeill*: 45. *Cavendish Square Publishing, LLC Royalty Free*: 39. *Newscom*: Mark Conlin/V&W, 22-23. *Photo Researchers*: Bernard Edmaier, 38. *Photoshot*: D. P. Wilson, 10; Tom & Therisa Stack, 42-43. *Tips Images*: Karen Jettmar/Alaska Stock, 26-27.

Printed in the United States of America

Contents

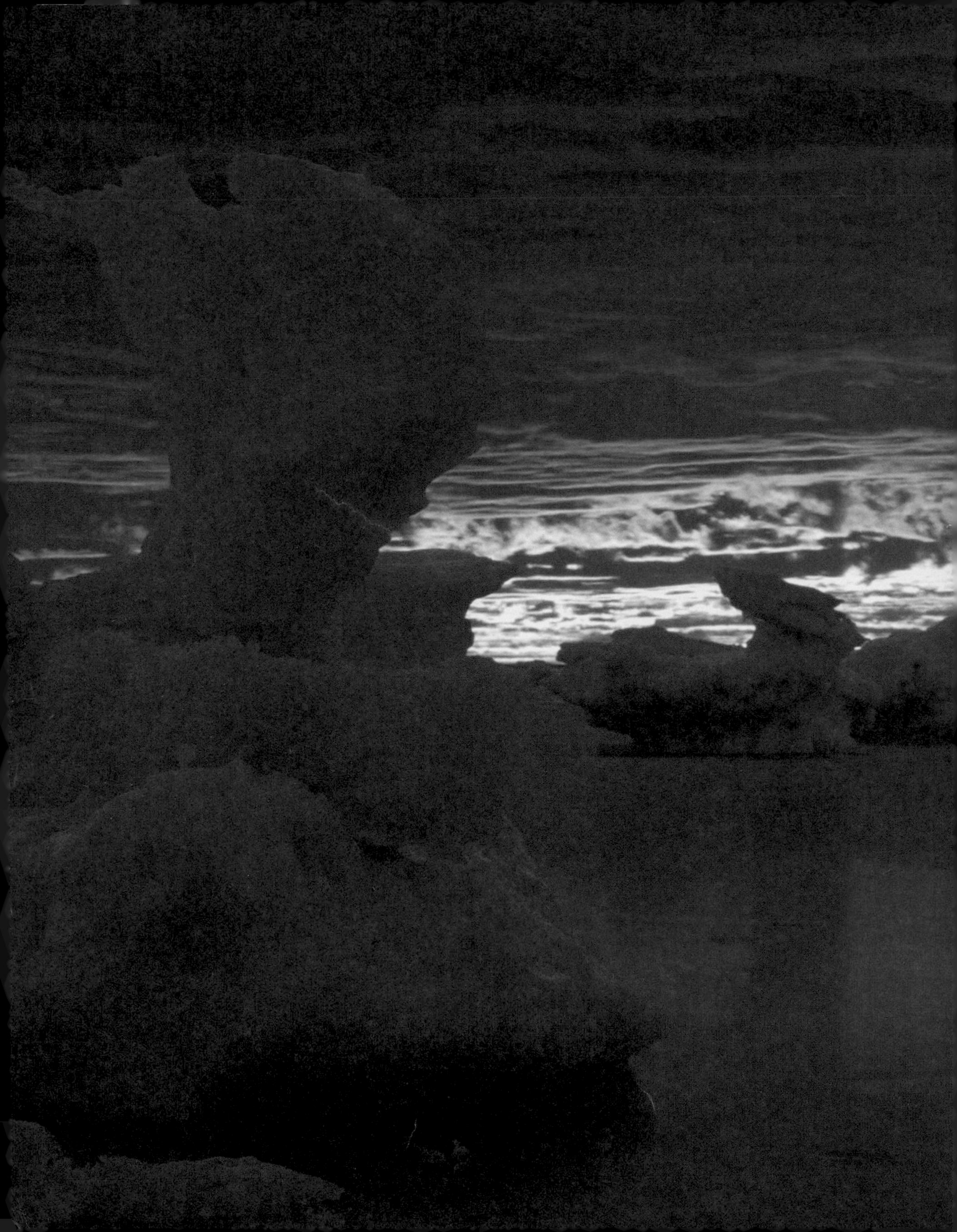

Introduction

ithout the ocean, our planet would be a very different place. Not only does the ocean absorb excess heat, it produces about half of the oxygen for the air we breathe, making the Earth habitable. What many people don't know is that the ocean significantly reduces global warming by storing much of the **carbon dioxide** (CO_2) produced by human activities.

The ocean covers 71 percent of the surface of our planet and plays an enormous role in the regulation of global climate. Surface currents distribute warm water around the world like a giant radiator, actively regulating temperatures and rainfall patterns. Water vapor rises up from the ocean to the atmosphere, creating clouds, rain, sleet, and snow. In this way the ocean drives the global water cycle.

Many scientists believe that life originated in the ocean, yet to this day, more than 95 percent of the underwater world is still largely unexplored. There are only 230,000 known marine life forms but scientists estimate that the total number of species could be a million or more. Scientists are just now becoming aware of the enormous impact that climate change is having on ocean life, and ultimately, all life on Earth.

Only 1.5 percent of the ocean has been protected, compared to over 12 percent of land areas.

A crimson sunset of Hudson Bay casts a dramatic purple light on the ice floes near Churchill, Manitoba, Canada.

The Ocean Conveyor Belt

Despite the fact that we have named five major ocean bodies—the Atlantic Ocean, the Pacific Ocean, the Indian Ocean, the Arctic Ocean, and the Southern Ocean—the ocean is actually one continuous body of water, wrapping around the continents and other land masses.

The ocean is constantly in motion. Winds create currents on the surface, while differences in water temperature and salinity (saltiness) create currents deep underwater. Both types of currents circulate the ocean water around the world. This global network of interconnected currents and countercurrents is known as the ocean conveyor belt.

The conveyor belt is crucial to the global climate. Without its moderating influence on Europe, Paris would have roughly the same climate as the Hudson Bay area in Canada—and that is cold! Also, the nutrient transfer that occurs from the mixing of deep ocean waters with surface layers is vitally important for phytoplankton growth. This takes place during a process called **upwelling**, part of the movement of the conveyor belt.

In Greenland in the North Atlantic, dry, cold winds chill the surface waters that, along with evaporation and sea-ice formation produce cold, salty North Atlantic deep water. Salty, or saline, water is denser and therefore heavier, while freshwater is more buoyant and floats closer to the surface. The deep North Atlantic water sinks further down and flows southward along the coast of North and South America toward Antarctica and then eastward, mixing with the waters of the Southern Ocean near Antarctica. The resulting water then flows northward into the Pacific and Indian Oceans, where it warms and mixes with the overlying waters. In the Pacific and Indian Oceans the warming water rises to the surface and eventually enters the

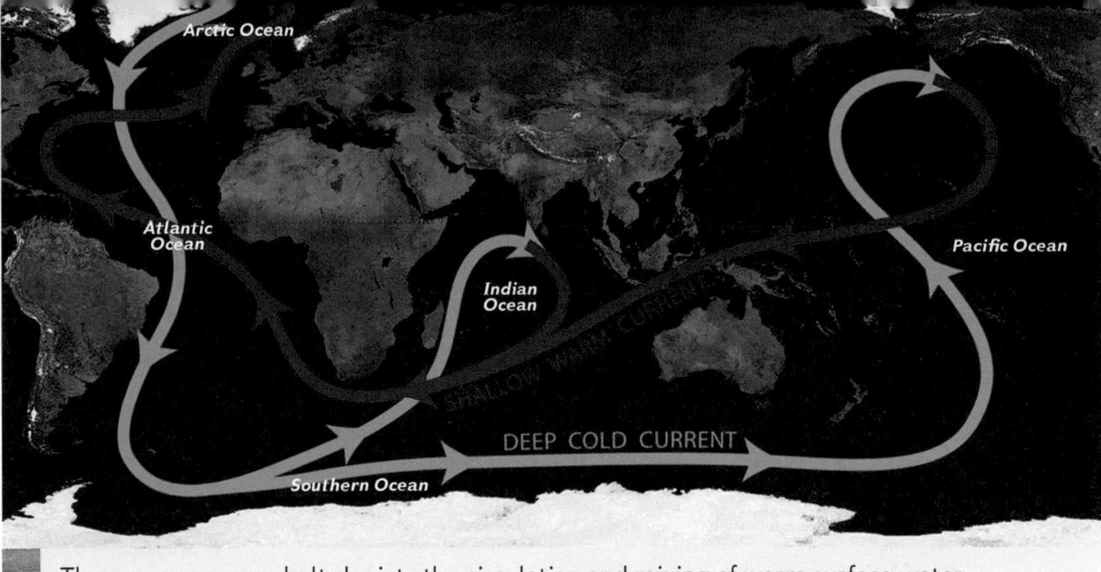

The ocean conveyor belt depicts the circulation and mixing of warm surface water (red arrows) and cooler deep-ocean water (blue arrows).

Agulhas Current that flows around southern Africa. After entering the Atlantic, the water joins the wind-driven currents and becomes saltier due to evaporation by the tropical sunlight. The water eventually returns to the Labrador and Greenland seas.

The moderation of northern Europe's climate takes place as warm waters flow northward through the Gulf Stream and the North Atlantic current. During a period known as the Little Ice Age (1400 to 1850 CE), warm waters ceased to flow north, resulting in a much cooler European climate. The conveyor belt, for some unknown reason, appeared to have temporarily switched off, and climatologists are concerned that this may happen again.

The conveyor belt is expected to slow down in response to climate change. In a warmer world, more rain will fall in the Polar Regions and sea ice and glaciers will melt, increasing the proportion of freshwater in the oceans. Increased freshwater is expected to slow down the pattern of currents and thus the mixing of ocean water layers. This will disrupt the flow of nutrients through the ocean system, particularly through the Southern Ocean. There is evidence that this is already taking place.

A wide variety of colorful fish and corals are found in this tropical coral reef in the South Pacific near Fiji.

Chapter One

Marine Life in a Warming Ocean

A wide variety of creatures live in the ocean, from microscopic algae beneath Antarctic ice floes, to the largest and loudest animal ever to live on Earth, the blue whale. Marine ecosystems range from colorful, sunlit coral reefs in tropical oceans to deep ocean ecosystems where the light of day barely reaches. Yet many marine food chains remain quite simple—as simple as the biggest feeding on the smallest. The gentle whale shark, for example, the largest living fish, swims slowly through surface waters consuming plankton, crustaceans, and small fish, filtering them through its large mouth like a giant marine vacuum cleaner. But scientists are finding that such simple food chains can also be very vulnerable.

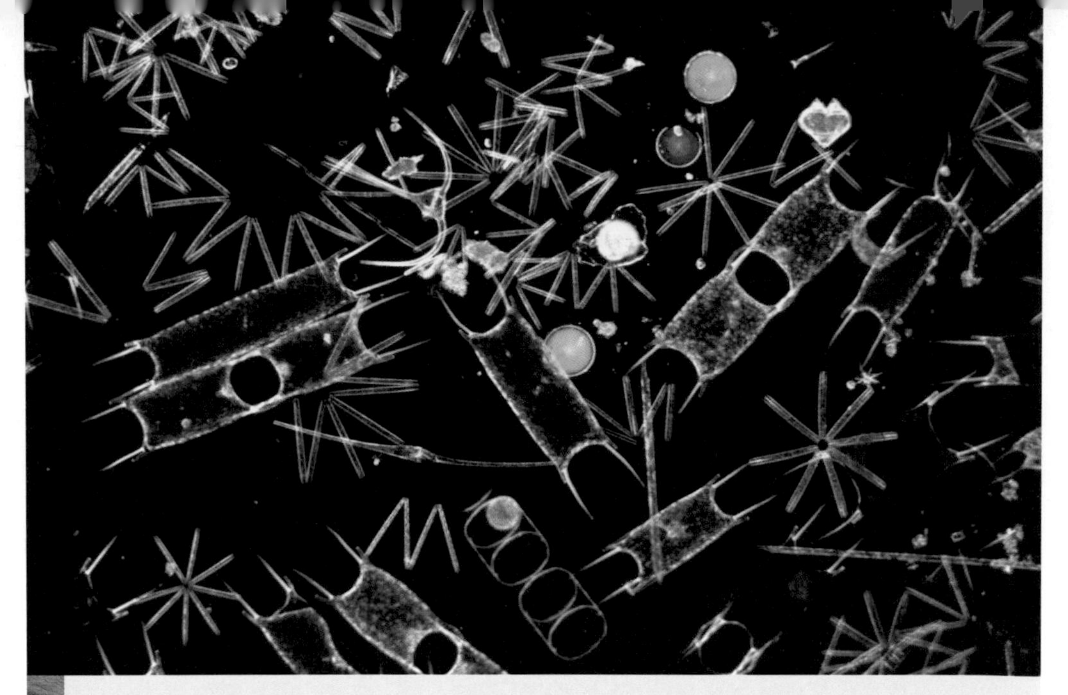

Though tiny, phytoplankton come in many different shapes. They are crucial for the production of oxygen and the absorption of carbon dioxide from the atmosphere.

An increase in ocean water temperatures due to climate change is affecting the very base of the marine food chain. Those organisms that live near the surface, where the water is more strongly affected by temperature changes, are often the first to feel the heat.

The ocean has absorbed more than 80 percent of the heat added to the global climate system since the recording of data started in 1961.

Plankton

A million of them can live in a single teaspoon of seawater, yet the ocean's amazing phytoplankton produce half of the oxygen in our atmosphere—as much as all the terrestrial (land-based) forests combined! Floating freely on the surface layers of the water, these tiny one-celled plantlike organisms convert the sun's energy through photosynthesis into plant material so they can grow.

Recording Plankton Levels

The Continuous Plankton Recorder is a device that allows researchers to take sea-wide samples of plankton. It has been active in the North Atlantic Ocean since 1931, when the recorder was invented by explorer Alister Hardy. This specialized box, which is dragged behind commercial ships, has been used as part of the Continuous Plankton Recorder Survey to measure plankton levels in the North Atlantic.

The information gathered with the Continuous Plankton Recorder, along with air temperature records, provides the most comprehensive climate–ecosystem set of data recorded for any ocean. The records show that as temperatures have changed, so has every part of the food web, starting with the plankton that are at its foundation.

In contrast to land plants that can live several months—or thousands of years in the case of some trees—the entire global phytoplankton **biomass** is consumed every two to six days. This makes plankton an excellent indicator of environmental change. Phytoplankton grow faster in a cool ocean and slower in a warm one so water-temperature changes directly affect the phytoplankton levels. NASA satellites take photographs of the ocean, which scientists assess to determine where phytoplankton growth is taking place and therefore whether ocean waters are warming or cooling. The greener the ocean water, the higher the level of phytoplankton growing there. In this way scientists can track ocean temperatures.

By absorbing carbon dioxide from the atmosphere, large populations of phytoplankton can have a powerful effect on the global climate. Phytoplankton can help lower carbon dioxide levels in the atmosphere and, in turn, keep the global temperature in check. As temperatures rise, phytoplankton reproduction goes down and therefore less carbon dioxide is absorbed. As a result, carbon dioxide accumulates more rapidly in the atmosphere and global temperatures rise even more. Clearly, these unsung heroes are vital to the health of our oceans and to all life on Earth.

A warmer ocean means surface layers become "lighter" than the cold, dense, nutrient-rich layers below. This separates phytoplankton on the upper surface layers from their nutrients below, resulting in reduced growth.

Zooplankton are the tiny animal counterparts of phytoplankton. They feed on phytoplankton and they are in turn eaten by other ocean creatures such as mussels, fish, birds, and whales. Zooplankton range in size from tiny viruses and bacteria that are invisible to the human eye, to huge jellyfish up to 6 feet (2 m) in diameter and weighing 25 pounds (11 kgs) or more.

Did you know that it snows in the ocean? Carbon (C)—a highly stable chemical element that is found in all living things and in coal and charcoal—enters the ocean when carbon dioxide is absorbed by phytoplankton during photosynthesis. This carbon then passes along to zooplankton and other predators through the food chain. The resultant **organic matter**, which is denser than seawater, sinks further down in the ocean, carrying the carbon with it. These tiny particles sinking through the middle layers of the ocean are known as **marine snow**. As the "snow" decays, much of the carbon dioxide is released back into the water when it combines chemically with water molecules (H_2O). But a significant amount of marine snow and the carbon it contains becomes buried in the ocean sediment, making the ocean the largest **carbon sink** on Earth.

Global warming is also causing marine dead zones, areas where fish and other sea life suffocate from lack of oxygen, to spread across the world's tropical oceans. Researchers have found that warmer seawater has less ability to carry dissolved oxygen, resulting in more frequent dead zones.

Fish

Whether nibbling on coral polyps, skimming plankton on surface waters, or probing the muddy ocean floor, thousands of species of fish inhabit marine ecosystems all over the world. But warmer waters, as well as changing rainfall patterns, currents, and sea levels, are affecting these fish populations and the fisheries they sustain. Rising **greenhouse gas** emissions threaten at least three quarters of key fishing grounds.

Since fish are cold-blooded, every aspect of their **physiology** is controlled by external temperature. Each species is adapted to live within a certain thermal range. Temperatures at the high end of this range cause metabolic inefficiency: fish living at these higher temperatures simply cannot eat enough food to supply their energy demands. On the other hand, temperatures at the lower end of the range cause a decrease in activity and appetite, leading to a reduction in growth and weight gain.

TIME TO ACT fact!

NASA compared satellite data of ocean phytoplankton levels with global climate records, such as changes in sea surface temperature, and found that whenever ocean temperatures warmed, phytoplankton declined.

Fish are, in effect, caught between a rock and a hard place. Not only are fish appetites affected by warmer ocean temperatures, but so are their food sources. Along with less available oxygen, warmer waters are known to produce less food for fish, resulting in stunted growth and fewer offspring. Some fish, such as salmon, catfish, and sturgeon, cannot spawn (reproduce) at all if winter temperatures are not cold enough. These changes can cause instability and collapse of ocean ecosystems. What other changes in marine life can we expect if temperatures keep increasing?

Fish populations may relocate to cooler waters in an effort to find their preferred temperatures. There are indications that some species are shifting **ranges** already. Other marine organisms that depend on these species as a food source may be left behind to starve. There are also indications that more than half of the world's species of sharks and rays may be in danger of extinction as a result of the compounding pressures of overfishing and climate change.

A strange thing is happening in the Sea of Japan. In recent years, giant jellyfish—orange-red blobs the size of tractor tires—have inundated this ocean region. This is another indication that our oceans may be completely changing in their composition due to climatic change, and at an extremely rapid rate. Computer models indicate that in the future marine species of fish will shift toward the poles an average of 25 miles (35 km) per decade. Many species will not cope well with this shift, and, in some cases, they may be threatened with extinction.

In 1993 the Gulf of Alaska became too warm for many indigenous (native) fish species, so some species moved into deeper, cooler waters, with disastrous results. Close to 120,000 seabirds starved to death, unable to dive deep enough to reach their relocated prey.

CASE STUDY

THE BERING SEA

The northern region of the Bering Sea, which is located between Siberia and Alaska, is typically covered with ice for seven months of the year. The ice is melting earlier, and the region appears to be shifting from arctic to subarctic conditions. The warming waters are interfering with the phytoplankton life cycle, resulting in fewer clams and worms on the ocean floor. This spells trouble for gray whales, walruses, and seabirds.

Large pods of gray whales from Baja California travel north to find cold water and food. Many are now traveling farther north to the Chukchi Sea, which is above the Arctic Circle, looking for colder waters and food sources. Some of the whales are so comfortable in the northern waters that they are now only returning as far south as Kodiak, Alaska.

However, the gray whale's northward shift is putting them close to the territory of the quieter and less aggressive bowhead whale, and possibly to that of the endangered North Pacific right whale that also swim north to the Bering Sea to feed. There are only about three hundred North Pacific right whales left. It is not yet clear how the right whales will respond to the warming waters, but there is no doubt that the Bering Sea waters are changing.

A southern right whale breaks through the ocean's surface waters in a behavior known as breaching.

Krill

TIME TO ACT fact!

Krill populations have declined by as much as 80 percent in key areas of the Antarctic.

Krill, tiny shrimplike crustaceans, are probably the most successful animal species on the planet, in terms of total biomass. They are also the favorite food of many of the great **baleen whales** in the Antarctic. An adult blue whale can consume more than 4 tons of krill a day on its annual Antarctic visit. Krill are dependent on Antarctic sea ice, since they feed on algae living on the bottom of the ice during the harsh winter months. But krill populations are in decline due to rising temperatures and melting sea ice. Scientists are concerned that whale populations may disappear, along with the ice. Researchers are also relating reduced krill availability to a decline in Antarctic fur seal pups, which often depend on krill as a prime food source.

Marine Mammals

Climate change is affecting cetaceans (marine mammals such as whales, dolphins, and porpoises), and the greatest impact is occurring in the Arctic and Antarctic regions. Reduced sea ice is expected to dramatically affect belugas, narwhals, and bowhead whales that rely on icy, polar waters for their **habitat** and food resources. Climate change could also be the final blow for the last three hundred or so endangered North Atlantic right whales. As oceans warm, the plankton and small fish upon which the whales feed are moving farther north, threatening long-term feeding and migration patterns.

Studies show that female sperm whales have lower rates of conception after periods of unusually warm sea surface temperature.

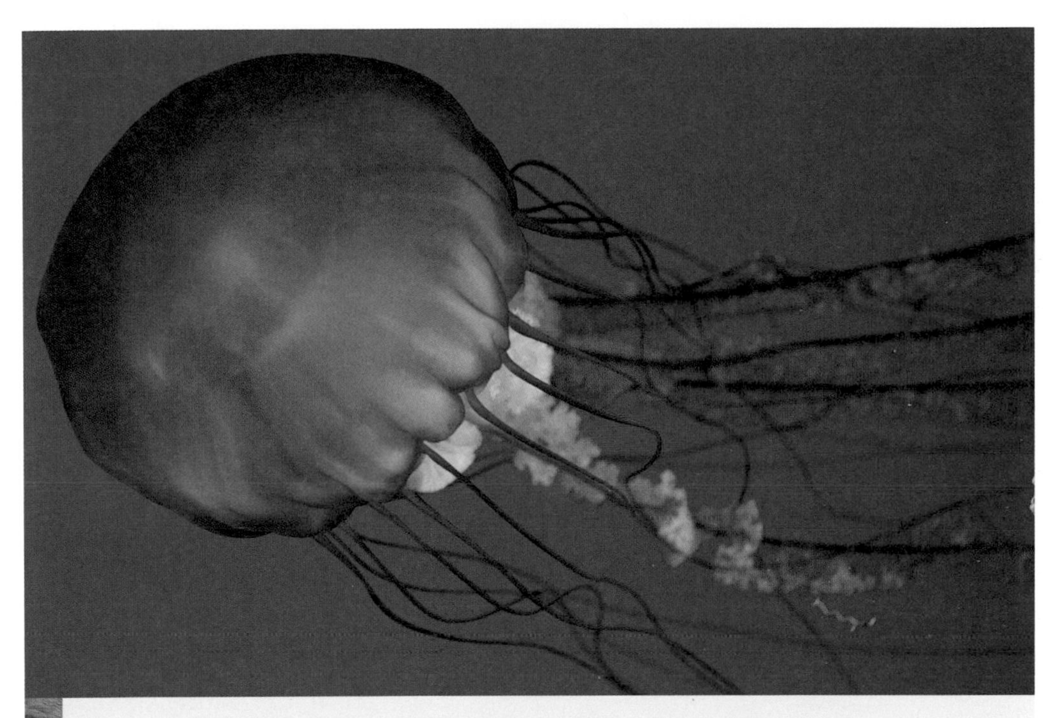

A Pacific sea nettle jellyfish. Changes in jellyfish populations can indicate changes in ocean temperature.

Coral Reefs

Rich patches of emerald and aquamarine sparkle in the shallow waters of the tropics, fringing islands and atolls, and wrapping continental coastlines like colorful ribbons. These coral reefs occupy less than 0.1 percent of available space on Earth, but they are home to one-quarter of all marine species. Often referred to as "rain forests of the sea" because they are the most productive and biologically diverse of all marine ecosystems, coral reefs have existed for 50 million years. Today, scientists monitor the vulnerable corals as indicators of global change.

Bleached staghorn coral off the coast of Australia. Warmer ocean waters have caused an increase in the incidents of coral bleaching, threatening reefs all over the world.

A reef consists of hundreds of thousands of soft-bodied, invertebrate (spineless) animals called coral polyps. These polyps build reefs by extracting calcium from seawater and building calcium carbonate cases to house themselves and the algae that help to nourish them. These shells store and cycle carbon dioxide and, therefore, contribute to the **pH** balance of the ocean. Growing on top of the stony skeletons of previous colonies, reefs provide habitat for tens of thousands of species, from bacteria and algae to manta rays and sharks. Reefs that grow near islands or mainland areas also protect coastal zones and mangroves from rough ocean waves and they nurture fisheries in the bays they create. Many unique medicines have been derived from reef species, and the reefs also provide recreational and tourism opportunities.

Unfortunately, warm ocean waters can kill the algae part of corals, causing the casing to appear white, or bleached. The loss of the algae also results in weaker corals that are more susceptible to disease. Reef ecosystems had

What Is Coral Bleaching?

As ocean temperatures rise, corals are losing some or all of their color—bleaching completely white. Coral tissues are actually clear. The beautiful coral colors come from the single-celled algae called *zooxanthellae* that live in **symbiosis** with the coral polyps. The algae provide nutrients to the coral in the daytime through photosynthesis, and at night the corals open up to feed on tiny plankton in the water. The coral polyp in return provides a protected environment for the algae as well as a steady supply of carbon dioxide.

Warmer waters are now affecting the ability of the algae to photosynthesize. Ultimately, the coral loses the algal organism that provides both its color and the majority of its food. If the water temperature remains too high for the algae to return, the coral dies. Even if the algae return, often the coral is weakened and susceptible to disease. Coral vulnerability to bleaching varies between species. Staghorn coral, one of the most vulnerable groups, has been listed by the National Oceanic and Atmospheric Administration as threatened under the Endangered Species Act.

CASE STUDY

THE GREAT BARRIER REEF

Australia's Great Barrier Reef is the world's largest living organism, stretching out for more than 133,000 square miles (345,000 km^2). With more than 2,900 reefs and approximately 900 islands, the Great Barrier Reef is also the world's largest and most complex coral reef system. Warming ocean waters are threatening its health after being battered by other threats such as coastal development, poor water quality due to coastal runoff, and illegal fishing. The Great Barrier Reef, which has been productive for millions of years, could be functionally extinct within a few decades. Mass coral bleaching events took place in 1998 and again in 2002, at which time bleaching occurred on close to 60 percent of the reefs.

By 2030 deadly coral bleaching could be an annual occurrence if waters keep warming. Dugongs, marine turtles, seabirds, black teatfish, and some sharks have already declined significantly, while coral diseases and outbreaks of pests like the crown-of-thorns starfish, appear to be increasing in frequency. Can we sit back and let the world's greatest coral reef systems disappear in our lifetime?

already been weakened by pollution from chemicals and fertilizers, predatory species, and destructive fishing practices, but now warming ocean waters are pushing some reefs into the highly endangered category.

Most corals are limited to water temperatures between 64 and 89 °F (18 and 32 °C). Water temperatures above this limit often result in coral bleaching.

Warming seas all over the world have led to many bleaching events in the last few decades. The worst to date was during the extreme **El Niño** episode of 1998 in which at least 46 percent of the coral reefs in the Indian Ocean were lost. At St. Croix in the Caribbean, bleaching occurred as deep as 150 feet (46 meters). In 2005, high summer and fall sea temperatures caused extensive bleaching of reefs in the Florida Keys and farther south all the way to Barbados.

One study in 2006 focused on the reefs near the Seychelles—islands north of Madagascar in the Indian Ocean—and revealed that coral cover was dramatically reduced, less than a quarter of what it had been only ten years earlier. Fish diversity also decreased drastically with the reduction of their reef shelter.

Already 20 percent of coral reefs on Earth are damaged beyond recovery. The loss of reefs will have a catastrophic impact on all marine life, since reefs are not only the fundamental architecture of entire ecosystems, but are home to a large number of diverse species.

Leatherback turtles, the largest living marine reptiles, like to lay their eggs above the high-tide line. Rising sea levels are eroding many of their nesting sites. This newly hatched leatherback makes its way to the sea.

Chapter Two

Ocean Acidification

The increase in global carbon dioxide emissions is not only trapping heat in the Earth's atmosphere, it is threatening the very chemistry of the ocean waters! The human-made carbon dioxide in the atmosphere is largely a result of the burning of **fossil fuels** and the process involved in the production of cement. The ocean absorbs about half of the carbon dioxide generated from fossil fuel emissions, but the resulting dissolved carbon dioxide forms **carbonic acid** in seawater. This is the leading cause of the rise in ocean acidity.

Researchers predict that if carbon emissions continue at the current rate, ocean acidity will more than double by 2100. Studies show that this will result in oceans low in calcium carbonate, slowing growth and making shells and skeletons weaker in some marine species. The impacts of this acidity will vary by ecosystem and by region, but it is expected to be most severe for coral reefs and the Southern Ocean.

After 20 million years of stable ocean chemistry, in the last 250 years the ocean absorbed an estimated 530 billion tons of carbon dioxide, causing a 30 percent increase in ocean acidity.

The ocean has already absorbed substantial amounts of carbon dioxide. Have we reached an irreversible level of ocean acidification? Coral reefs and marine life, already under threat due to warming waters, will be under additional stress with increased acidity. Rebalancing the pH of the ocean could take thousands, or even hundreds of thousands of years.

Gut Rocks

There appears to be a link between oceanic fish populations and calcium carbonate levels, making fish an important ally against ocean acidification—and it all comes down to fish excrement called "gut rocks." Bony fish excrete lumps of calcium carbonate that dissolve in the upper layers of the ocean. This buffers the carbon dioxide that acidifies seawater and helps to maintain the delicate pH balance. Management of our ocean fisheries—including the prevention of overfishing and fish-stock depletions—is an important line of defense in the fight against climate change.

Marine Species

Arctic ringed seals need sea ice to rear their young pups. As a warming climate causes the sea ice to retreat, the seals are being forced farther north. This causes problems for beluga whales, which prey on the seals. They must also move north to follow their food source. The retreating sea ice, therefore, disrupts an entire food chain! Belugas, highly sociable mammals, are also vulnerable to ship strikes and pollution, both of which are likely to increase as the retreating sea ice opens up areas of the ocean, making gas and oil exploration in the Arctic more feasible.

- Emperor penguins, highly adapted to the Antarctic environment, are also facing troubles as their sea-ice habitat shrinks. They rely on the sea ice for mating, moulting, and rearing their chicks.
- In tropical waters staghorn corals, comprised of some 160 species, are severely affected by rising ocean temperatures due to the risk of coral bleaching. Also, ocean acidification, from high levels of carbon dioxide in the water, weakens the external skeleton surrounding the coral polyps.
- Clownfish are also vulnerable to ocean acidification. Acidic water impairs their acute sense of smell, which they rely on to find refuge in their specific host anemone.
- Rising sea levels and increased storm activity are destroying the nesting habitats of leatherback turtles. Temperature increases may also lead to a reduction in the proportion of males relative to females. This gender imbalance can lead to eventual extinction as males are gradually eliminated from the gene pool.

The Hubbard Glacier in southeast Alaska's Disenchantment Bay calves, or releases ice chunks, into the water, contributing to sea-level rise.

Chapter Three

Rising Sea Levels

Sea level changes are not a new phenomenon. They have occurred throughout the history of Earth. During the peak of the last ice age 20,000 years ago, sea levels were much lower than they are now because so much of the water was frozen and stored on land. But sea levels have been rising since the start of the nineteenth century at a much more rapid rate, ten times faster than in the past 3,000 years. One worrisome fact hangs over these changes: for every half inch (1.3 cm) that the sea rises, more than 3 feet (1 m) of coastal land is lost to the sea.

There are several reasons that sea levels rise. The first is a process known as thermal expansion—the increase in volume (and decrease in density) when water is heated. Since the ocean is like a bathtub with no drain, the increase in volume of warming ocean water causes sea levels to rise. Simple fact!

The melting of ice on land is the second most important cause of rising sea levels. Glaciers and ice sheets cover about 10 percent of the world's land area, and they are found on every continent except Australia. Computer models predict that sea levels will continue to rise at an increased rate into the next century.

TIME TO ACT fact!

Melting of glaciers and ice caps in this century is expected to raise sea levels an additional 4 to 5 inches (10 to 12 cm). This represents a melting of a quarter of the total amount of ice tied up in mountain glaciers and small ice caps.

The melting of sea ice and floating icebergs, on the other hand, do not affect sea levels due to Archimedes' Principle: an object totally or partially immersed in water is lifted up by a force that is equal to the weight of water it displaces. In other words, ice in the ocean has already displaced its mass of water, so the sea level does not rise when it melts.

The average global temperature has increased 1.3 °F (0.74 °C) over the past century. If this trend continues, and we have every reason to believe that it will, thermal expansion will contribute more than half of the sea-level rise in the next century. Land ice will also lose mass at an increasing pace as temperatures rise through the century. The Arctic is warming at a rate faster than the global average, so increasing surface melt from the Greenland Ice Sheet is expected.

So why the big concern over sea levels anyway? Well, one of the greatest impacts of rising sea levels could very well be on people. Ten percent of the world's population (an estimated 600 million people) live very close to the sea. Bangladesh is arguably the most vulnerable country in the world to sea-level rise because most areas rise less than 30 feet above sea level and the country is regularly inundated by storm surges and severe flooding. In this country of more than 150 million people, 17 million live less than 3 feet (1 m) above sea level. A 3-foot (1-m) rise in sea level could be catastrophic.

Structures to protect coastlines would have to be built for many major cities, including New York, London, Mumbai, and Shanghai. Seawater flooding creates a risk of disease and results in a reduction in the quality and quantity of freshwater. Some species and ecosystems that cannot adapt quickly enough to changes in salinity could be lost forever.

Large rises in sea levels could wreak havoc on coastal regions important for trade ports, fisheries, agriculture, and tourism. Also, rising sea levels would suppress coral growth and perhaps deal the final blow to reef ecosystems already under pressure from warming waters and ocean acidification. In addition, nursery habitats (places where the young of certain species mature) are flooded by sea level rise, affecting the ability of many marine organisms to reproduce.

CASE STUDY

THE FIRST CLIMATE CHANGE REFUGEES?

The evacuation of entire populations has already started from certain Pacific Ocean atolls that are losing ground to rising seas, and is being considered for others.

The Carteret Islands are part of Papua New Guinea (PNG) in the South Pacific. The islanders have fought in vain for more than twenty years against the rising ocean, building sea walls and planting mangroves. Salt water intrusion into homes and gardens is a growing problem during storm surges and high tides. Homes have been washed away, vegetable gardens destroyed, and freshwater supplies contaminated. It is not entirely clear if the submersions are solely the result of climate change–induced sea-level rise, but it certainly is a contributing factor.

In 2005, the government of Papua New Guinea authorized the evacuation of the Carteret Islands' nearly 1,000 residents, ten families at a time, to Bougainville, another PNG island. The evacuation started in 2007. It is estimated that by 2015 the Carteret Islands could be largely submerged and entirely uninhabitable—a painful example of the real impact of rising sea levels. The people of the

Carteret Islands may go down in history as the first climate change refugees. A similar fate awaits the small nation of Tuvalu and Majuro in the Marshall Islands.

Tuvalu, an island nation in the Pacific, is at risk of disappearing if sea levels continue to rise.

A polar bear and her two small cubs on an ice floe in the Arctic Ocean. Arctic sea ice is melting rapidly due to warming temperatures

Chapter Four

Polar Oceans

Something extraordinary happened at the top of our planet in the past few years. In the final days of the summer a large stretch of open water appeared around the Arctic. This made it briefly possible to pilot a ship from the Atlantic to the Pacific Ocean without going through the Panama Canal or around the Cape of Good Hope. Never before in recorded human history has it been possible to make that journey.

The polar ice caps are the Earth's refrigerator. They reflect a lot of the sun's heat and help to keep the Earth cool. Without polar ice we would have a dramatically warmer world. However, the ecosystems in the Polar Regions are delicate ones. The loss of one keystone species could have alarming impacts.

Of the many changes that have taken place in the world's climate over the past two decades—and there have been a lot—one of the most drastic has been the loss of ice around the world. Climate change in the Polar Regions is expected to be among the largest and most rapid of any region on Earth, causing major physical, ecological, sociological, and economic impacts.

Greenland has lost 1.5 trillion tons of ice since the year 2000 and is now melting at a rate double that of 2002—a dramatic change in less than a decade. Antarctica has lost 1 trillion tons of ice since 2002.

The Arctic Ocean

Arctic inhabitants cannot help but notice the changes in their world. Spring thaws are earlier and fall freeze-ups are later. Sea ice is shrinking. Unfamiliar plants and animals are popping up, as if out of nowhere. Migratory birds are arriving earlier and leaving later, and some have never been seen in this part of the world before. To make matters worse, intense storms are more frequent than ever. In the words of Alaska native Hudson Sam:

> It was a lot colder when I was young, months at a time. This weather nowadays is unpredictable; it just comes and goes anytime it wants to.

Temperatures in the Arctic Region rose an average of 2.5 °F (1.4 °C) between 1999 and 2008, a very short period of time in terms of climate history! The Intergovernmental Panel on Climate Change (IPCC) found that over the last one hundred years the average annual temperature in the Arctic has increased almost twice as fast as the global increase. It is no surprise that data from the U.S. National Snow and Ice Data Center (NSIDC) indicates

The Catlin Arctic Survey

On March 1, 2009, a team of rugged polar explorers got together with some of the world's best scientists. They set out to solve one of the most important environmental questions of our time: how long will the Arctic Ocean's sea ice cover remain a permanent feature on Earth?

To answer this question they needed solid data, so they decided to literally dig out the truth. The Catlin Survey team tackled the harsh Arctic climate to take detailed measurements of ice thickness and density in order to accurately determine the length of time the ice will remain.

The surprising result of their data is that the survey area was comprised almost exclusively of first-year ice. This is significant because the region has traditionally contained a larger proportion of older, thicker, multi-year ice. The average thickness of the ice floes, at less than 6 feet (1.8 m), was considered too thin to survive the following summer's melt.

The Polar Ocean Physics Group at the University of Cambridge analyzed these findings and concluded that the Arctic will be ice-free in summer within about twenty years. This means that by 2030, Arctic sea ice may disappear altogether during the summer months.

Two members of the Catlin Survey team take an ice core sample.

that Arctic sea ice is in a state of ongoing decline, throughout *all* months. This decline is greater—and its rate faster—than can be explained by any natural causes!

Polar bear populations in the western part of Hudson Bay have declined by 22 percent, and the numbers are dropping elsewhere too. If summer Arctic ice disappears, the polar bear may follow.

The loss of Arctic sea ice cover could set in motion powerful climate feedbacks with impacts far beyond the Arctic itself. The dark ocean waters will absorb more heat from the sun, increasing Arctic temperatures further. This will increase melting of the Arctic permafrost, ground that is frozen year round and that stores twice as much carbon as the atmosphere. In addition, the frozen arctic seafloors—home to more carbon than in all of Earth's known reserves of coal, oil, and natural gas combined—may begin to melt as well. One of the biggest fears is that the loss of sea ice will accelerate melting of the Greenland Ice Sheet, speeding up the global rise in sea level.

Polar bears need sea ice to hunt seals, their main prey. With ice declining and breaking up earlier in the spring, the polar bear's hunting season is becoming dangerously short. The legendary bear was listed as a threatened species under the U.S. Endangered Species Act in May of 2008. There are about 25,000 polar bears left in the wild, and more than 60 percent of them live in the Canadian Arctic. Wouldn't it be a cruel crime against nature and future generations if we cannot save the magnificent polar bear?

Other Arctic animals also depend on the sea ice. Pacific walruses, which typically plow the ocean floor looking for clams and other prey, have started gathering near the shore and on land. The sea ice, which walruses use as a resting platform between dives, is extending beyond their reach as the ice rapidly retreats northward. In addition, in areas where the sea ice remains, the sea floor is often too deep for adult walruses to feed. Ringed seals, ivory gulls, and ice algae also rely on the sea ice to survive.

The people of the north are suffering the impacts of a warming world. Many northern communities are watching helplessly as the permafrost melts and buckles under their homes and roads. Less sea ice also means that ocean waves travel farther over open water and gain strength before breaking on Arctic shores. Shorelines, weakened by melting permafrost, are vulnerable to erosion from these crashing waves. Some Alaskan communities, like Kivalina and Shishmaref—where the coastline has eroded 100 to 300 feet (30 to 90 m) in the past thirty years—are planning to relocate entirely, with estimated costs in the hundreds of millions of dollars.

Antarctica

The Southern Ocean surrounds Antarctica, and this isolation has prevented large land predators from reaching the Antarctic Peninsula. Thus, many animal species, such as the emperor penguin, use Antarctica as both a breeding ground and a winter refuge, unmolested by wolves, bears, or other carnivores.

However, human activities such as seal hunting, whaling, and fishing have had major impacts on the Southern Ocean and Antarctica. And now climate change poses an additional threat, causing changes to the number and distribution of many species. For example, migratory patterns of whales, such as the humpback and the minke, may change as populations of one of their preferred foods, krill, decline with the melting ice.

On a larger scale of change, in 2002 glaciologists watched in amazement as a 1,250-square-mile (3,250-km^2) section of the huge, 10,000-year-old

CASE STUDY

GREENLAND ICE SHEET

The Greenland Ice Sheet—the second largest ice body in the world after the Antarctic Ice Sheet—contains 10 percent of the world's freshwater. In some places the ice sheet is about 2 miles (3 km) thick.

Glaciologists in Greenland are almost as common as reindeer these days. They are busy studying why the ice sheet is melting and why it is moving so much faster than expected. Like slippery fingers inching seaward, the ice sheet has rapidly increased the speed with which it stretches down into the fjords, pushing ice into the ocean in the form of meltwater and icebergs. Kangerdlugssuaq, a glacier on the eastern side of the ice sheet, is moving at a speed of 1 inch (2.5 centimeters) per minute—visible to the naked eye!

Most scientists working at the poles predict sea levels will rise more than 3 feet (1 m) by the end of the century. The IPCC predicted in 2007 that the sea level will rise 1 to 2 feet (30 to 60 cm) by the end of the century. But if *all* the ice in the Greenland Ice Sheet melted, sea levels would rise by an estimated 23 feet (7 m)!

The Greenland Ice Sheet inches its way to the sea

Emperor penguins are the largest of all living penguin species. As temperatures have risen, their populations have decreased.

Larsen B Ice Shelf in Antarctica collapsed into the ocean. Even more surprising was the speed of the breakup—less than three weeks! The very next year, Argentine glaciologists reported that the land-based glaciers exposed by the removal of those sections had surged rapidly toward the ocean.

All of this newly open water is resulting in changes to the food web. Adélie penguins, a species well adapted to sea-ice conditions, have declined in number and chinstrap penguins, an open-water species, are rising in number.

CASE STUDY

PINE ISLAND, ANTARCTICA'S FASTEST MOVING GLACIER

British scientists wanted to find out what was happening in one of the remotest areas of our planet. So in the winters of 2006–2007 and 2007–2008, they camped out on the West Antarctic Ice Sheet in some of the harshest weather on Earth. These scientists are trying to figure out why one particular section of it—Pine Island Glacier—is melting so much faster than the rest.

Pine Island Glacier is 95 miles (153 km) long and 18 miles (29 km) wide, reaching the sea as a wall of ice almost half a mile (1 km) high. Even before it began to speed up, Pine Island was one of the fastest-flowing glaciers in the world, at 27 feet (8 m) a day. Researchers from the British Antarctic Survey (BAS) theorize that the glacier is melting and accelerating due to warm waters from the North Atlantic that are driven into the Southern Ocean by strong currents.

Underwater regions near glaciers are extremely dangerous places, so the BAS designed a remotely controlled submarine. The Autosub will enter the hazardous underwater world beneath the glacier and, using sonar, will map out the 40-mile (64-km) journey to the place where the ice meets the land.

Understanding glacier movements in Antarctica is vital for future predictions of climate change. Glacial melt in this region of the world will be a big factor in determining how much our sea levels rise. Saving the glaciers has become a critical battle in the fight against climate change.

Seals and emperor penguins, famous for their role in the film *March of the Penguins*, are also decreasing in population size, apparently due to warming seas, reduced summer sea ice, and lack of krill, their prime food.

It's not just animals that are affected by the effects of climate change on Antarctica. Plants have started to colonize soil by spreading their seeds and seedlings on areas once permanently covered by snow and ice. Compared to our knowledge of the continent's plants and animals, we know very little about Antarctica's microbial (microscopic) life. When the Larsen B Ice Shelf collapsed, scientists discovered a rich deep-sea ecosystem, a community of clams, and a thin layer of bacterial mats flourishing in undersea sediments. Invisible to the naked eye, these bacterial organisms play a vital role in Antarctic ecosystems. They are rich but untapped resources, perhaps containing the components for new antibiotics and other medicinal compounds.

Analysis of global measurements of atmospheric carbon dioxide indicates that the Southern Ocean carbon sink has weakened significantly since 1981. This reduction in the capacity of the ocean to absorb carbon dioxide has been attributed to increased upwelling of carbon-rich waters associated with strengthening of the westerly winds. Although future changes in the ability of the Southern Ocean to absorb carbon dioxide can be only partly predicted, this will be a key factor that helps shape global climate.

Student volunteers transplant harvested corals onto a damaged portion of Conch Reef, which is located off the coast of Key Largo, Florida.

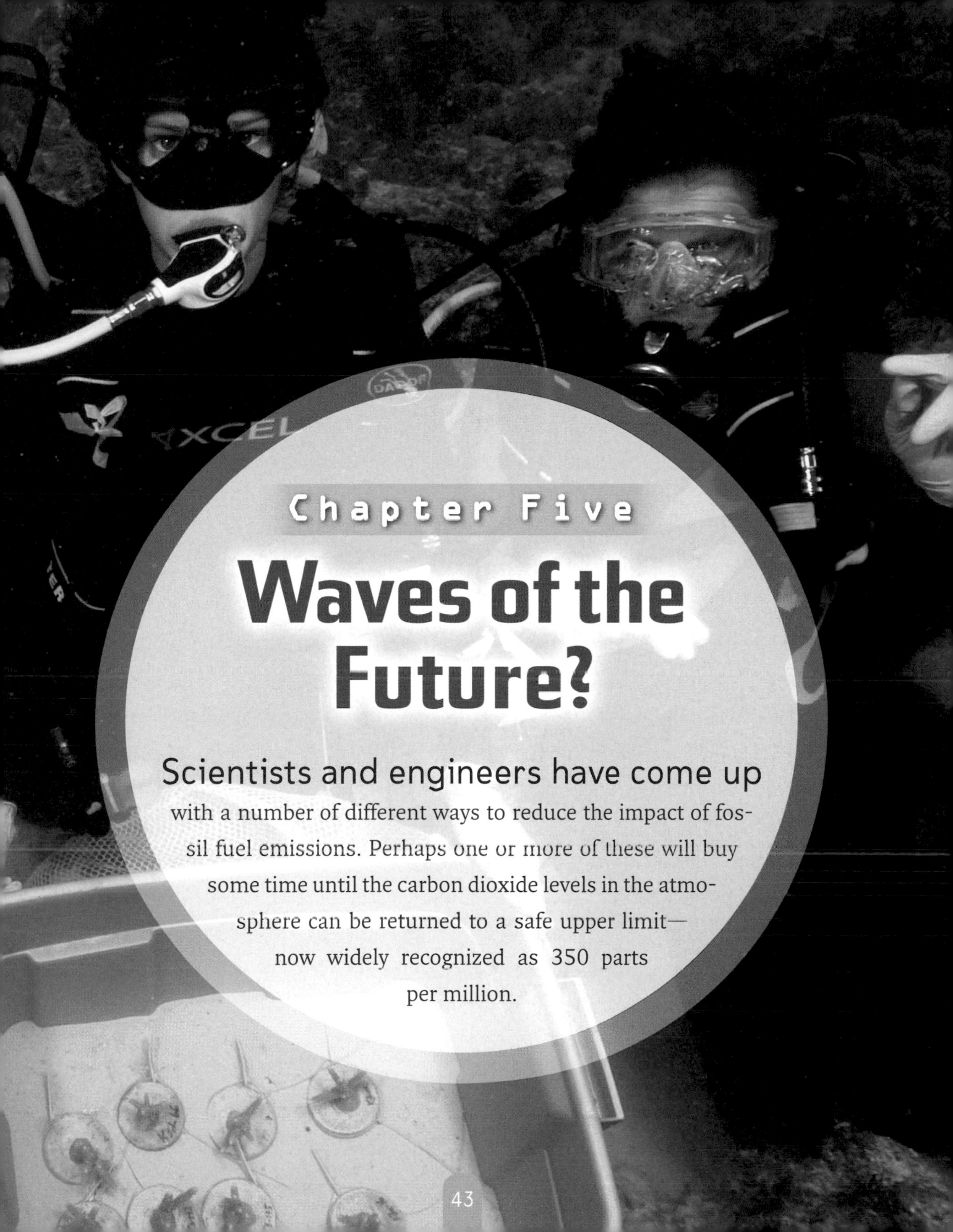

Chapter Five

Waves of the Future?

Scientists and engineers have come up with a number of different ways to reduce the impact of fossil fuel emissions. Perhaps one or more of these will buy some time until the carbon dioxide levels in the atmosphere can be returned to a safe upper limit—now widely recognized as 350 parts per million.

(Parts per million, or ppm, is simply a way of expressing how many carbon dioxide molecules there are for every one million total molecules in the atmosphere.) Of course, none of these ideas should substitute for the pursuit of international legislation on carbon emissions or other means to reduce fossil fuel emissions—a must if we are to keep our planet habitable for the future.

Making use of the great ability of the ocean to absorb carbon dioxide is an obvious place to start in the battle against global warming. If phytoplankton levels in the low-nutrient areas of the ocean are increased, more carbon dioxide could be absorbed from the atmosphere. But what effect would this have on the overall marine environment?

Deep-Sea Pumps

Researchers have designed deep-sea pumps that will bring the nutrient-rich, deep-sea water to the surface, where phytoplankton live, feed, and breed. The pumps use wave energy to bring up water from as far down as 900 feet (300 m) below the surface. By nourishing the population of carbon dioxide-absorbing phytoplankton, the scientists hope to create a model that can be expanded into a large-scale geoengineering project.

Other scientists worry about the consequences of changing the ocean environment in such a massive way since we understand so little about the oceanic checks and balances. Will too many nutrients brought up from the deep result in uncontrolled plankton blooms? This is a big problem in many coastal regions where there is a lot of nutrient runoff into the sea, which also fuels plankton blooms. There are many questions still to be answered before this technology leaves the development stage.

Ocean Fertilization

Scientists have shown that experimental additions of iron, an essential **micronutrient** for phytoplankton, create almost instantaneous growth in phytoplankton populations. Even iron-rich dust storms, blown from land over the sea, can create plankton blooms. Some laboratory experiments suggest that every ton of iron added to the ocean could remove 30,000 to 110,000 tons of carbon from the air through absorption by phytoplankton. Numbers like this make it apparent why some people are eager to sprinkle iron on the seas. Others fear that there could be other consequences—aside from decreasing the amount of carbon in the air and increasing the amount stored in the ocean—that scientists have not considered.

There are many ways that additional iron might actually harm the ocean. There could be side effects from the added iron itself, direct effects from plankton growing and decomposing, indirect effects on other nutrients cycling through the ocean, and unexpected physical effects of more plankton being packed into surface waters. Also, when a plankton bloom runs its course and the organic material that it produces sinks to deeper waters, the resulting bonanza of decomposition typically uses up oxygen in the water. Such low-oxygen conditions can cause significant die-offs in fish, shellfish, and invertebrates. Clearly, ocean fertilization experiments must be approached with extreme caution, and until the results can be more accurately predicted, large-scale approaches should be prohibited entirely.

Cloud-Seeding Ships

The idea of manipulating clouds is not a new one—scientists made the first attempt in 1946. By firing tiny particles of silver iodide (a substance used in photography) into rain-bearing clouds, rainfall was induced. Now, researchers have developed plans to increase the albedo (reflectivity) of clouds, and therefore reduce the amount of sunlight reaching the Earth. To accomplish this, they have designed a cloud-seeding ship that propels seawater droplets into the air. This wind-powered, unmanned vessel is remotely guided to regions that will benefit from the cooling effect of the cloud cover. By spraying fine droplets of seawater into the air, the small particles of salt within each droplet act as new centers of condensation when they reach the clouds

Cloud seeding is not a new idea, but advances in technology are helping scientists move toward efficient cloud-seeding ships that may slow climate change.

above. This is expected to create a greater concentration of water droplets within each cloud so the cloud will reflect more sunshine. Less sunshine on the ocean surface means cooler waters.

The inventors calculate that about 1,000 cloud-seeding ships would be required to make the plan effective. The ships could be sent to coral reefs, polar ice sheets, or other vulnerable regions. According to the theories, due to the great thermal-heat capacity of the ocean and the currents within it, the cooler waters would eventually spread across the globe.

One of the great strengths of this proposal is that it requires only seawater as a raw material. Research is still needed to determine if there could be any harmful climate side effects, such as reduced rainfall in regions where water is already scarce.

Cruising for a Plug-in

There will be no more idling engines in Vancouver's harbor. Alaska-bound cruise ships reaching Canada's biggest port will now be able to get their power while in dock from the city's electricity grid. This shore power facility allows the ships to cut their engines and therefore reduce the overall diesel emissions for their journey, improving local air quality in the harbor area at the same time. The electric harbor is the third of its kind in the world. Let's hope this is a growing trend.

Injecting Carbon Dioxide into the Ocean

Direct injection of excess carbon dioxide into ocean waters has been suggested by some as a possible way to prevent it from reaching the atmosphere. However, estimating the impact of carbon injection is difficult. Ocean circulation can change, thereby affecting the amount of time carbon is stored in the deep ocean. Also, studies show that climate change has a big impact on the ocean's ability to store carbon dioxide. Eventually this stored carbon dioxide could percolate to the surface and into the atmosphere.

Finding a safe storage place for harmful materials, as nuclear-energy proponents have discovered, is not so easy. Modeling shows that certain locations in the ocean will hold carbon much longer than others. But which ocean region will future climate change have the least effect upon? That's difficult to determine. Hiding carbon in the deep ocean is, at best, a strategy to buy time. At worst, it could hamper the ocean's existing carbon-carrying capacity.

Nursery-Grown Corals

Scientists at the National Coral Reef Institute (NCRI) in Florida are growing their own corals from the larval stage so that they can transplant them into damaged coral reefs. The NCRI is evaluating this technique to raise and restore populations of staghorn, mustard hill, and great star corals. Indoor aquaria harbor the immature corals until they are ready to be relocated to the outdoor coral system. If the corals grow successfully enough in the outdoor system, they will be transplanted into damaged reefs. Brilliant idea! Doesn't it feel good to know that science is helping our coral reefs fight back against the destructive impacts of climate change?

Unlike in a chemistry or biology laboratory, where multiple controlled experiments can be conducted, we can't afford to perform large-scale experiments on global climate. If the outcome of an experiment with our climate system goes wrong, the consequences could be devastating. We are already living within an unintentional experiment on our planet: the rapid increase of atmospheric greenhouse gases and **aerosols** from burning fossil fuels and cutting down forests. We are living right inside the test tube! Climate experiments need to be approached with extreme caution so that we don't cause more damage.

However, scientific innovation *can* help minimize atmospheric levels of carbon dioxide until we have reached a global agreement to stabilize greenhouse gases. In the meantime there will be many opportunities both for new ideas and inventions, as well as for participation in the promotion and development of renewable energy sources and alternative technologies.

Members of a high school environmental club in northern New Jersey are collecting old cell phones to send to a recycling center.

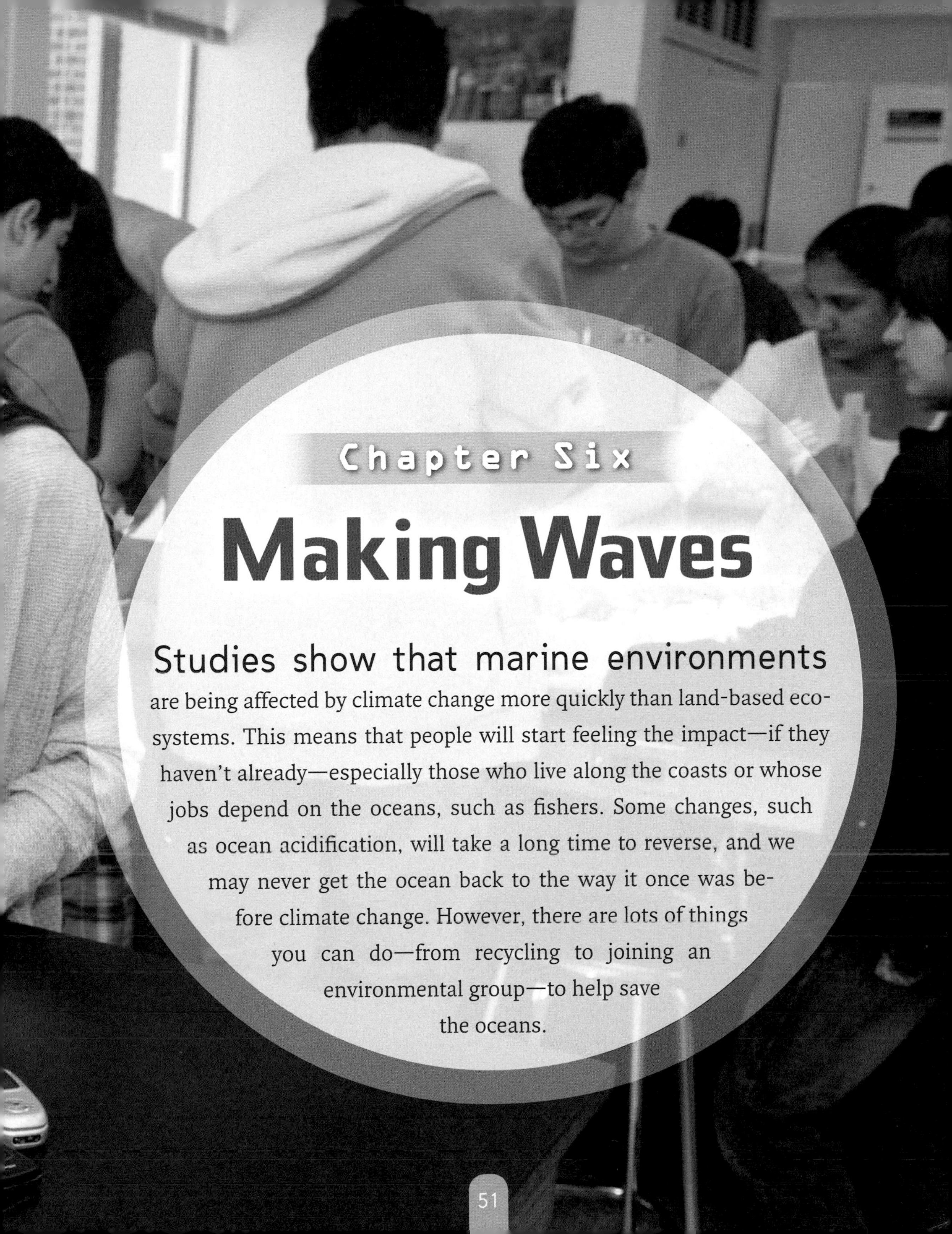

Chapter Six

Making Waves

Studies show that marine environments are being affected by climate change more quickly than land-based ecosystems. This means that people will start feeling the impact—if they haven't already—especially those who live along the coasts or whose jobs depend on the oceans, such as fishers. Some changes, such as ocean acidification, will take a long time to reverse, and we may never get the ocean back to the way it once was before climate change. However, there are lots of things you can do—from recycling to joining an environmental group—to help save the oceans.

You can get involved right now! One of the best starting points is to understand what is taking place in our oceans and to talk about it with others, such as your friends, family members, and classmates. Find people who are concerned about these matters too, and who want to make a difference. Talk to others about starting a "Save the Oceans" environmental group at your school.

BE A SMART SHOPPER

- Whether you're shopping for food, clothes, or other items, try to keep the environment in mind.
- Look for products made from recycled materials. These items reduce the need to harvest more natural resources, which means fewer greenhouse gases are emitted.
- Purchase sustainably farmed vegetables, fruits, fish, and meats. Sustainable agriculture improves the environment, uses resources efficiently, and works with natural biological cycles. Your local farmers' market is a good place to find sustainably farmed foods.
- Check out consignment shops for inexpensive and unique clothing. Most stores sell cool vintage pieces and unworn or lightly worn clothing and accessories.
- Buy wood products that have the FSC logo. This means that they are accredited by the FSC, or Forest Stewardship Council, an organization that certifies only products whose manufacture does not endanger the world's forests.

RECYCLE AND REUSE

- Recycling reduces the need for landfills and incinerators, and it conserves natural resources. Many products we use today can be recycled, including aluminum cans, plastic containers, paper, and clear glass. Recycling items means fewer greenhouse gas emissions are produced in the harvesting and manufacturing of natural resources. Check with your town or city to find out what the recycling procedures are for your area. Many retailers and organizations offer programs to recycle cell phones, computers, and other electronics so that they don't end up in landfills.

- Composting is a great way to put yard trimmings and food by-products that normally end up in the trash, such as banana peels, to good use. Compost naturally enriches soil, reducing the need for chemical fertilizers, which can pollute the ocean. Also, the manufacture of chemical fertilizers releases greenhouse gases that contribute to climate change.
- You can also help the environment and slow climate change by finding new uses for old items, such as using an empty glass bottle as a flower vase. This keeps items out of landfills, thus reducing greenhouse gas emissions.

USE LESS ENERGY

- Little changes in your daily life, such as using energy-efficient light bulbs, might not seem like much, but when lots of people make these changes the effect is significant. Carpooling or taking public transportation reduces the amount of greenhouse gases being emitted into the air. Even air-drying your clothes instead of using a dryer saves energy, which means fewer greenhouse gas emissions.

GET INVOLVED

- If you'd like to do more to combat climate change, consider joining an environmental group. Check and see if there is an environmental club at your school and, if not, ask a teacher to help you start one. You will meet classmates who are also concerned about the environment and want to work together to make a difference.

- You can also look at what programs in your school promote the reduction of fossil fuel emissions. Most schools have a recycling program that includes paper, glass, aluminum, and plastic. Encourage your classmates to recycle, since all of these products can end up littering habitats. If your school has a cafeteria, look at how the food is packaged. Are the containers recyclable? If not, ask a teacher to help you find out if it's possible to use recyclable containers.

- You can help prevent the extinction of a species by working with other people who have a lot of experience in conservation. Join an environmental organization that helps protect animals and their habitats. Three excellent organizations are:

  350.org—www.350.org

  Global Warming.com—www.globalwarming.com

  Will Steger Foundation—www.willstegerfoundation.org

  Check out these websites to learn how you can join!

Like waves in the ocean, our combined individual actions can create a powerful force, a force that can propel a tide of change toward creating a planet with healthy, sustainable, living oceans.

Glossary

aerosols Tiny particles suspended in the air; some occur naturally and others by human activities.

atoll An island of coral encircling a lagoon (an area of shallow seawater).

baleen Horny, bonelike substance that hangs down in plates from the upper jaws of baleen whales and is useful in filtering out krill from the water.

biomass The combined weight of all species of plants and animals in a given ecosystem; usually measured in weight per unit area, such as 50 pounds of squirrels per 3 square miles.

carbon dioxide A gas in the earth's atmosphere formed from two oxygen atoms bonded to a carbon atom. Chemical formula: CO_2.

carbonic acid The acid formed when carbon dioxide dissolves in water. Chemical formula: H_2CO_3.

carbon sink A natural or human-made reservoir that stores carbon or carbon-containing compounds for an indefinite period of time.

crustacean A marine arthropod with a hard exoskeleton, such as crabs and lobsters.

ecosystem A group of living and nonliving things that interact with each other.

El Niño An irregular, recurring flow of unusually warm surface waters traveling from the Pacific Ocean toward and along the western coast of South America.

fossil fuels Coal, oil, and natural gas; made from the remains of plants and animals that lived up to 300 million years ago.

greenhouse gas A gas, such as carbon dioxide, that prevents heat from escaping Earth's atmosphere, contributing to global warming.

habitat The natural environment in which a species lives.

ice floes Frozen, flat masses of seawater that float freely on the surface of the sea.

marine snow A continuous shower of organic debris from upper to lower layers of the ocean.

micronutrient A nutrient that a living thing needs in small quantities.

organic matter Material from a once-living organism that will eventually decay into its carbon-based components.

pH A measure of the acidity or basicity of a solution; a pH below 7 is an acid solution and above 7 is a basic, or alkaline, solution.

physiology The natural processes of a living thing.

plankton Small plants (phytoplankton) and animals (zooplankton) that drift near the water surface.

range The geographic location where a species naturally lives.

symbiosis A mutually beneficial relationship between two species often resulting in a long-term association.

upwelling The movement in the ocean whereby warm surface water, usually nutrient-depleted, is replaced by dense, cooler, and usually nutrient-rich water from below.

Notes

p. 5, "There are only 230,000 . . .": W. Appeltans et al., eds., *World Register of Marine Species*, www.marinespecies.org.

pp. 6–7, "In Greenland . . . Greenland seas": Edwin Schiele, "Ocean Conveyor Belt Impact," *Ocean Motion and Surface Currents*, NASA, http://oceanmotion.org/html/impact/conveyor.htm.

p. 7, "There is evidence that . . .": NASA, "Satellites Record Weakening North Atlantic Current Impact," NASA News and Events, April 15, 2004, www.nasa.gov/centers/goddard/news/topstory/2004/0415gyre.html.

p. 10, Time to Act Fact!: *IPCC Fourth Assessment Report: Climate Change 2007 (AR4)* (Geneva, Switzerland: United Nations Intergovernmental Panel on Climate Change, 2007).

p. 12, "As a result, carbon dioxide . . .": Michael J. Behrenfeld et al., "Climate-Driven Trends in Contemporary Ocean Productivity," *Nature* 444 (2006): 752–755.

p. 13, "Global warming is also causing . . .": Lothar Stramma et al., "Expanding Oxygen-Minimum Zones in the Tropical Oceans," *Science* 320 (2008): 655–658.

p. 13, "But warmer waters . . .": Stacey Combes, *Are We Putting Our Fish in Hot Water? Global Warming and the World's Fisheries*, World Wildlife Foundation report (Gland, Switzerland: WWF), 2005.

p. 13, "Rising greenhouse gas emissions . . .": C. Nellemann, S. Hain, and J. Alder, eds., *In Dead Water: Merging of Climate Change with Pollution, Over-Harvest, and Infestations in the World's Fishing Grounds*, Rapid Response Assessment, United Nations Environment Programme (UNEP) (GRID-Arendal, Norway: UNEP, 2008).

p. 13, Time to Act Fact!: David Herring, "What Are Phytoplankton?" NASA Earth Observatory, http://earthobservatory.nasa.gov/Features/Phytoplankton/.

p. 14, "Fish populations may . . .": William W. L. Cheung et al., "Large-scale Redistribution of Maximum Fisheries Catch Potential in the Global Ocean Under Climate Change," *Global Change Biology* 16, no. 1 (January 2010): 24–35; and Richard R. Kirby and Gregory Beaugrand, "Trophic Amplification of Climate Warming," *Proceedings of the Royal Society B* 276 (December 7, 2009): 4095–4103.

p. 14, "There are also indications that more . . .": Nicholas K. Dulvy et al., "You Can Swim But You Can't Hide: The Global Status and Conservation of Oceanic Pelagic Sharks and Rays," *Aquatic Conservation: Marine and Freshwater Ecosystems* 18, no. 5 (May 2008): 459–482.

p. 14, "Close to 120,000 seabirds . . .": John Piatt and Thomas Van Pelt, "Mass-Mortality of Guillemots (*Uria aalge*) in the Gulf of Alaska in 1993," *Marine Pollution Bulletin* 34, no. 8 (August 1997): 656–662.

p. 15, "It is not yet clear . . .": Jacqueline M. Grebmeier et al., "A Major Ecosystem Shift in the Northern Bering Sea," *Science* 311 (2006): 1461–1464.

p. 16, Time to Act Fact! (top): W. Elliott and M. Simmonds, *Whales in Hot Water? The Impact of a Changing Climate on Whales, Dolphins and Porpoises: A Call for Action*, World Wildlife Foundation and the Whale and Dolphin Conservation Society (Gland, Switzerland: WWF-International, 2007).

p. 16, "Researchers are also relating . . .": Jaume Forcada et al., "The Effect of Global Climate Variability in Pup Production of Antarctic Fur Seals," *Ecology* 86, no. 9 (January 2005): 2408–2417.

p. 16, "Climate change is affecting . . .": J. Turner et al., "Antarctic Climate Change During the Last 50 Years," *International Journal of Climatology* 25 (2005): 279–294.

p. 16, Time to Act Fact! (bottom). W. Elliott and M. Simmonds, *Whales in Hot Water? The Impact of a Changing Climate on Whales, Dolphins and Porpoises: A Call for Action*, World Wildlife Foundation and the Whale and Dolphin Conservation Society (Gland, Switzerland: WWF-International, 2007).

p. 18, 21, "Reef ecosystems had . . .": R. W. Grigg and S. J. Dollar, "Natural and Anthropogenic Disturbance on Coral Reefs," In *Coral Reefs*, ed. Z. Dubinsky (Amsterdam, Netherlands: Elsevier, 1990), 439–452.

p. 19, "Warmer waters are . . .": B. E. Brown and J. C. Ogden, "Coral Bleaching," *Scientific American* 268 (1993): 64–70.

p. 20, "The Great Barrier Reef, which has been . . .": *IPCC Fourth Assessment Report: Climate Change 2007 (AR4).*

p. 20, "Mass coral bleaching events . . .": WWF-Australia, "Great Barrier Reef," World Wildlife Fund, http://wwf.org.au/ourwork/oceans/gbr/.

p. 21, "One study in 2006 . . .": Nicholas A. J. Graham et al., "Dynamic Fragility of Oceanic Coral Reef Ecosystems," *Proceedings of the National Academy of Sciences* 103 (2006): 8425–8429.

p. 23, "This is the leading cause . . .": United Kingdom, The Royal Society, Science Policy Section, *Ocean Acidification Due to Increasing Atmospheric Carbon Dioxide*, 2005.

p. 24, "Researchers predict . . . Southern Ocean.": James C. Orr et al., "Anthropogenic Ocean Acidification Over the Twenty-first Century and Its Impact on Calcifying Organisms," *Nature* 437 (2005): 681–686.

p. 24, Time to Act Fact!: Natural Resources Defense Council, "Ocean Acidification: The Other Carbon Dioxide Problem," Issues: Oceans, September 17, 2009, www.nrdc.org/oceans/acidification/.

p. 24, "Management of our ocean fisheries . . .": R. W. Wilson et al., "Contribution of Fish to the Marine Inorganic Carbon Cycle," *Science* 323 (2009): 359–362.

p. 25, "Rising sea levels . . .": Sarah Horsley, ed., *Species and Climate Change: More Than Just the Polar Bear*, IUCN Species Survival Commission report (Gland, Switzerland: IUCN, 2009).

p. 28, "Computer models predict . . .": *IPCC Fourth Assessment Report: Climate Change 2007 (AR4).*

p. 28, "The average global temperature . . .": *IPCC Fourth Assessment Report: Climate Change 2007 (AR4).*

p. 28, Time to Act Fact!: *IPCC Fourth Assessment Report: Climate Change 2007 (AR4).*

p. 30, "It is estimated that . . .": "Carteret Atoll," Global-Greenhouse-Warming.com, http://www.unesco.org/new/en/rio-20/single-view/news/i_need_a_new_home_my_island_has_sunk/.

p. 34, Hudson Sam quoted in Elliott and Simmonds, *Whales in Hot Water?*

p. 35, "The Catlin Survey team tackled . . .": N. P. Toberg and P. Wadhams, "Verification of Catlin Arctic Survey Surface Observation Techniques," Polar Ocean Physics Group, Department of Applied Mathematics and Theoretical Physics, University of Cambridge, 2009.

p. 37, "On a larger scale . . .": Lucinda Spokes, "Oceans and Climate," *Climate Encyclopaedia*, ESPERE Education Network on Climate, www.atmosphere.mpg.de/enid/5ddee7bd8785cc4bc22780eb67a92785,0/more/1__Oceans_and_climate_1vq.html.

p. 38, "The Greenland Ice Sheet . . .": Patrick Barkham, "The Sermilik Fjord in Greenland: A Chilling View of a Warming World," *The Guardian*, September 1, 2009, www.guardian.co.uk/environment/2009/sep/01/sermilik-fjord-greenland-global-warming.

p. 40, "British scientists wanted . . .": British Antarctic Survey, "Measuring One of the World's Largest Glaciers," British Antarctic Survey, Natural Environment Research Council, www.antarctica.ac.uk/bas_research/science/climate/pine_island_glacier/index.php.

p. 44, "Other scientists worry . . .": Discovery Channel, *Ways to Save the Planet*, "Phytoplankton," Discovery Channel International, http://news.discovery.com/earth/geoengineering-carbon-sequestration-phytoplankton.htm.

p. 46, "Clearly, ocean fertilization . . .": Aaron Strong et al., "Ocean Fertilization: Time to Move On," *Nature* 461 (September 17, 2009): 347–348.

p. 46, "Recent studies also indicate . . .": Raymond T. Pollard, "Southern Ocean Deep-Water Carbon Export Enhanced by Natural Iron Fertilization," *Nature* 457 (January 26, 2009): 577–580.

p. 46, "Now, researchers have . . .": Stephen Salter, Graham Sortino, and John Latham, "Sea-Going Hardware for the Cloud Albedo Method of Reversing Global Warming," *Philosophical Transactions of the Royal Society A* 366 (November 13, 2008): 3989–4006.

p. 47, "The electric harbor . . .": Nicole Mordant, "Vancouver Cruise Ships to Plug In to Cut Pollution," Reuters, August 31, 2009, www.reuters.com/article/idUSN3144824620090831.

p. 48, "But which ocean . . .": University of Illinois at Urbana-Champaign, "Climate Change Will Affect Carbon Sequestration in Oceans, Scientists Say," *Science Daily*, December 4, 2002, www.sciencedaily.com/releases/2002/12/021204080934.htm.

p. 48, "If the corals grow . . .": National Oceanic and Atmospheric Administration, "NOAA Helps National Coral Reef Institute to Grow Coral in Laboratory to Restore Damaged Reefs," NOAA News, February 28, 2008, http://www.noaa.gov/features/resources_0109/coralreefs.html.

Find Out More

Books

Cherry, Lynne, and Gary Braasch. *How We Know What We Know About Our Changing Climate: Scientists and Kids Explore Global Warming*. Nevada City, CA: Dawn Publications, 2008.

Foster, Karen. *Atlas of the Poles and Oceans*. Mankato, MN: Picture Window Books, 2008.

Geiger, Beth. *Our Changing Climate: The Poles*. San Diego, CA: Sally Ride Science, 2009.

Goldman, Laurie. *Our Changing Climate: The Oceans*. San Diego, CA: Sally Ride Science, 2009.

Guigon, Catherine. *The Arctic*. New York: Harry N. Abrams, Inc., 2007.

Hartman, Eve. *Climate Change*. Mankato, MN: Heinemann-Raintree, 2009.

Jakab, Cheryl. *Climate Change*. Mankato, MN: Smart Apple Media, 2008.

Lishak, Antony. *Global Warming: What's That Got to Do with Me?* Mankato, MN: Smart Apple Media, 2008.

Lourie, Peter. *Arctic Thaw: The People of the Whale in a Changing Climate*. Honesdale, PA: Boyds Mills Press, 2007.

Rhodes, Mary Jo, and David Hall. *Life on a Coral Reef*. Danbury, CT: Children's Press, 2007.

Sommers, Michael A. *Antarctic Melting: The Disappearing Antarctic Ice Cap*. New York: Rosen Publishing Group, 2007.

Wojtyla, Karen. *Shark Life: True Stories About Sharks & the Sea*. New York: Yearling, 2007.

Websites

Earth Child Institute (ECI)

ECI is committed to combating climate change, deforestation, and water scarcity by empowering the 2.2 billion people under the age of eighteen. There are programs for those interested in learning how to plant and care for a tree, getting involved with renewable energy technologies, cleaning up local environments, and more!
http://earthchildinstitute.org

EPA: Your Environment. Your Choice.

The EPA's campaign for teens is dedicated to providing information so that readers can make the most environmentally responsible choices in their day-to-day lives.
www.epa.gov/epawaste/education/teens/index.htm

Intergovernmental Panel on Climate Change

The IPCC, a scientific organization with thousands of scientists from all over the world, was established by the United Nations Environment Programme (UNEP) and the World Meteorological Organization (WMO). It is the leading organization for the assessment of climate change and the reports are available for free download from the website.
www.ipcc.ch

Oceanus Magazine

Oceanus is a magazine published by the Woods Hole Oceanographic Institution in Massachusetts that explores the oceans in depth. Its website provides information on a wide variety of topics in oceanography, including pollution, natural hazards, and issues related to climate change impacts on ocean life.
www.whoi.edu/oceanus/index.do

Sci Jinks

This site, run by NASA and the NOAA, is an instructional website aimed at students. It provides information and games about weather, the oceans, the atmosphere, and satellites and technology in a fun, kid-friendly format.
http://scijinks.jpl.nasa.gov

Index

Page numbers in **bold** are photographs, illustrations, and maps.

About the Author

Stephen Aitken is fascinated by the natural world and its remarkable diversity. He is the author of many books for young people from third grade to high school, written for publishers all over the world. Stephen is a biologist and senior editor of *Biodiversity*, a peer-reviewed science journal, and executive secretary of Biodiversity Conservancy International. He is a vegetarian, does not own a car, and tries to keep his carbon footprint as close to his shoe size as possible. Stephen's studio in the beautiful Himalayas of India provides shelter for ants and spiders, baby geckos, and an odd orange-eared mouse. For a complete list of books that Stephen has written and illustrated please visit: www.stephenaitken.com.